100 THINGS
TO KNOW ABOUT
ART

Quarto is the authority on a wide range of topics.
Quarto educates, entertains and enriches the lives of
our readers—enthusiasts and lovers of hands-on living.
www.quartoknows.com

Author: Susie Hodge
Illustrator: Marcos Farina
Editor: Emily Pither
Creative Director: Malena Stojić
Associate Publisher: Rhiannon Findlay

First published in 2021 by Happy Yak,
an imprint of The Quarto Group.
The Old Brewery, 6 Blundell Street,
London N7 9BH, United Kingdom.
T (0)20 7700 6700 F (0)20 7700 8066
www.quartoknows.com

A catalogue record for this book is available from the British Library.

ISBN 978-0-7112-6342-0

Manufactured in Guangdong, China TT062021

9 8 7 6 5 4 3 2 1

MIX
Paper from
responsible sources
FSC® C016973
FSC www.fsc.org

SUSIE HODGE   MARCOS FARINA

100 THINGS TO KNOW ABOUT ART

happy yak

CONTENTS

INTRODUCTION

What do you think of when you hear or read the word art? Paintings? Drawings? Pottery? Sculpture? Art is amazing, fun and fascinating. Artists from the past and present have created marvellous things for us all to see, from fabulous frescoes to intricate mosaics, from glittering glass to magnificent paintings, stunning sculptures and beautiful pots. Many materials that artists used in the past have been added to or replaced by new materials and ways of using them.

You can't sum up art in just a few words, and so this book is full of words and explanations about it – techniques, materials, ideas and inventions – probably everything you ever wanted to know about art is here! All you need to do, is to turn the pages and discover the wonderful world of art, from the ancient past to the present.

Be prepared to be inspired to make your own incredible art!

ACRYLICS

· ·

Used by artists since the 1960s, acrylic paint comes in squeezy tubes and hard 'cakes'. It comes in a wide variety of different colours and shades, from dark and deep, to light and bright. Invented in the 1950s, acrylics are made with plastic, so once dry, they become waterproof. When mixed with plenty of water, they can have watercolour-like effects, or mixed with less water, the paint is thick and can be made to look like oils. Acrylics dry far quicker than oil paints and can be used on many different surfaces, even those that are difficult to paint on.

BRONZE

Bronze has been the most popular metal for making
sculptures for about 4,000 years, using something called the 'lost-wax' process. For this, a clay
core is made for a sculpture. Wax is then moulded around it in the shape of the sculpture and is coated
with more clay, leaving a hole in the bottom. The whole thing is then heated so the wax melts and runs
out, leaving a space between the two lots of clay. Melted bronze is poured in and when it sets, the clay
is removed, leaving the finished sculpture which can be polished to a shine.

CHALK

Chalk is a soft kind of rock that is usually white, dry and crumbly.
Artists often use it on dark surfaces so that their light chalk marks stand out and can be seen.
Nowadays, chalk for artists is mainly made in special factories, but it is also still found in
the ground. Some ancient artists cut huge images into the ground, revealing the white chalk below.
For example, the Bronze Age White Horse at Uffington in Oxfordshire is a huge white
chalk horse carved into the green grass of a hill. The bold, horse shape can be seen for miles.

CHARCOAL

···

Charcoal is one of the oldest drawing materials – it has been used by artists since prehistoric times, tens of thousands of years ago. Prehistoric artists often used charcoal to paint on rocks and cave walls to create art, share stories and record ideas. Since then, it has been a popular material for drawing and sketching. It is brittle and black, and it can create soft or hard lines, or be smudged for shading and other effects. Charcoal is made from charred wood and can be used in sticks, inside pencils, as powder or compressed, which means it's thicker and firmer.

CLAY

Made up of tiny particles of rock, clay is a kind of earth.
Like many other minerals, clay is dug up from the ground and before it's used,
it has to be cleaned. When mixed with water, it can be pinched, rolled, cut, squashed
or pushed to form different shapes. As it dries, it hardens, and when baked in a kiln – a special
kind of hot oven – it becomes completely hard and long-lasting. Archaeologists have found
clay objects that are thousands of years old and artists today continue to create
many objects with clay, such as vases, pots and tiles.

CRAYON

A crayon is a pencil or stick of coloured chalk or wax
that is used for drawing or writing. Although the ancient Egyptians drew with coloured wax,
the crayons we know and use today were not invented until the 19th century. Because they're light,
fun to use, easy to hold and make bold, firm marks, they are often used by young children when they
start to draw. But crayons come in hundreds of exciting colours and are used by professional artists,
too. Crayons can be used in layers to make rich, deep colours, or with light pressure for
lighter colours.

GOUACHE

· ·

Gouache ("goo ash") is a non-see-through, water-based paint with a creamy consistency
and a matt finish. Gouache can be a really flexible paint – it is great for layering and blending and
can even mimic the look and feel of acrylic, watercolour and oil paints. Palette knives, sponges, paint
brushes, rags and even twigs can be used to create different effects and cool textures with gouache paint.
Often used by illustrators and graphic designers, it can be easier to use than watercolour paint,
simply because mistakes can be easily painted over! Dry gouache can sometimes be adjusted
with a wet brush.

INK

Made from earth, plant sap and even animal blood, early forms of ink
were used in some of the oldest cave paintings we know about, created more than
40,000 years ago. Around 4,500 years ago, people in ancient Egypt and China began
creating ink for writing. It was made from soot, mixed with gum or oil and water. They dipped in
sticks, brushes or birds' feathers, and wrote with this ink. Nowadays, ink is used by artists everywhere,
for things such as illustrations, pen and wash (ink and watercolour) and even printmaking.
Ink comes in a variety of different colours.

MARBLE

· ·

Marble is a limestone rock that can be polished to a smooth, dazzling shine.
As marble is easy to carve and is smooth to touch, it is popular with sculptors and has been used
to make amazing sculptures for thousands of years. Famous Renaissance artist Michelangelo used
a special white marble from a quarry called Carrara in Italy. Many other Italian Renaissance artists
preferred smooth white marble as it reminded them of ancient Greek and Roman statues.
Ancient sculptors often painted their marble statues but marble comes in many
patterns and colours, including white, black, grey, red, pink and green.

MIXED MEDIA

· ·

When different materials are used in one work of art, this is called mixed media.
The first famous artists to use mixed media were Pablo Picasso and Georges Braque in 1912,
while they were inventing a form of art that's now known as Cubism. They glued all sorts of
materials on their paintings, such as newspaper cuttings, photographs or pieces of fabric. We also
call this form of mixed media 'collage'. Another type of mixed media is 'multimedia art',
which is similar but includes 'new media' such as the internet, and can include
moving images or sound within the composition.

SHADING

· ·

To create the illusion of three-dimensions in a flat work of art,
artists often use a method called shading. Shading is all about building up dark
and light tones in a painting or drawing. It's achieved by using dark marks to represent
where the deepest shadows can be seen and leaving light areas or adding highlights to show where
the brightest light falls. Darker shading suggests that things are far away in the background or
deeper inside things, and lighter shading gives the impression that things are closer to
the surface of the image, or even sticking out from it.

SKETCH

Sketches are quickly completed drawings. They might be recordings
of things artists have seen, plans for future works of art or ideas that artists have thought of
and want to remember or show to others. Sometimes artists' sketches are called 'studies' or 'preparatory
drawings'. Made in almost any material, such as pencil, charcoal, pen, pastel, oil paints, gouache or
watercolour, and often on paper, most artists and designers make many sketches during their careers.
Sculptors often model 3D sketches in clay, plasticine or wax when planning their sculptures, and most
artists keep sketchbooks that they fill with sketches and ideas.

OILS

· ·

Oil paint is made by mixing dry powdered pigment with oil.
It was first used in Afghanistan in the 7th century. The first oil paintings seemed colourful
and glossy compared with earlier tempera paintings. As oil paint dries slowly, mistakes can be
corrected easily while it's still damp. Artists use oil paint in many ways to create different effects.
For example, with fine brush marks or thickly spread with a knife, applied in small broken marks,
thin layers or thick splodges. In most oil paintings, the darkest colours are applied first
and the lightest colours are added last, as highlights.

PASTEL

First used in Italy, pastels are sticks of powdered pigment mixed with a binder such as gum or resin. Although never as popular as oil paints, pastels became fashionable for portraits in Britain in the mid-18th century. By the late 1860s, French artists including Edgar Degas, Mary Cassatt and Henri de Toulouse-Lautrec used pastels to create new styles of colourful pictures. Soft or chalk pastel are the most commonly used types. Pastel colour glides smoothly onto paper and can be blended or smudged with your finger or special tools. Oil pastels, made with pigment, oil and wax, were invented later.

PENCIL

Pencils are fine sticks of graphite, clay and wax that are placed inside wood,
plastic or metal to make them easier to hold. Graphite was first discovered in the ground
in Cumbria, England. Local farmers used the graphite for marking their sheep as it was easy
to write with and showed up well on a sheep's white coat! The graphite in pencils is mixed with clay
and wax, and all pencils are graded from hard (H) to soft (B). The hardest, lightest pencil,
9H, has more clay, while the softest and blackest pencil
has more graphite and is graded 9B.

PIGMENT

· ·

Coloured powders used to make paint, crayons and pastels are known as pigments.
Ever since prehistoric times, natural pigments have been used by artists. Early pigments came
from things like rocks, stones or even crushed plants, flowers and fruits. Ultramarine (blue) for
example, came from semi-precious lapis lazuli stones, while verdigris green came from copper.
Later, some scientists began making pigments from chemicals and these pigments were brighter
and longer-lasting. To make art materials, pigments are mixed with a binder, such as oil, water,
wax or egg. The binder holds everything together and creates paint or things like coloured pencils.

TEMPERA

· ·

A fast-drying, long-lasting paint, tempera is made of pigment mixed with egg,
and was used by many artists for centuries before oil paint was invented. The colours
can be bright, but tempera dries with a matt finish and cracks easily after it has dried. Many
ancient artists in Egypt, Babylonia, Greece, Rome and China, as well as early Christian artists
painted with tempera. They usually painted it on different materials such as stone, wood panels,
ivory and papyrus. Some tempera was made with the yolk of fresh eggs,
some with just the egg white and some with the whole egg!

WATERCOLOUR

· ·

Both the paint itself and works of art made with the paint
can be described as watercolour. Watercolour paints come in small dry slabs
known as 'cakes' or as squeezy paste in tubes. They all need to be mixed with water
to be used as paint. Fairly see-through when dry, watercolours are usually used on thick paper that
won't crumple when it's wet! Sometimes, some parts of this white paper are left to show areas
of light. Watercolour artists use various techniques to create effects, such as wet-on-wet
(wet watercolour on wet paint) or wet-on-dry (wet watercolour over dry paint).

COLOUR

· ·

Colours are all around us. What colours can you see now?
How do they make you feel? Colours play a part in how we understand the appearance
of objects and scenes. We often describe a pink sunset, green grass or the blue sea. A colour wheel
is a circle divided into sections like a pizza. Each section is a different colour. It includes
primary colours: red, yellow and blue, and secondary colours: green, purple and orange.
Colours that are opposite each other on the wheel are known as complementary colours:
red and green, yellow and purple, and blue and orange.

COMPOSITION

The way the parts of pictures or designs are arranged is called the composition. Often, the whole of a work of art is described as the composition. Compositions can create different effects, for instance, horizontal lines often appear still and calm, while diagonal lines and bright colours make paintings seem lively and dynamic. Artists use all sorts of compositions, but some compositions are considered the most effective, such as images made up of three parts, or triangular compositions. For centuries, most pictures fitted completely inside their frames, but after photography was invented, some artists became more creative with their compositions.

CONTRAST

· ·

To create drama, artists often use contrast. This is usually areas of light and dark, but can
also mean contrasts of texture, such as rough and smooth, of lines, such as straight and wavy, or of
angles or shapes, such as circles and squares. Contrasts of light and dark are also often included to make
works of art look solid or dramatic. The lighter the light areas and the darker the dark areas, the more
3D or dramatic the art looks. In the image above, contrast has been used to show that the person
and dog are stargazing at night.

LINE

· ·

Lines are usually the first things we draw. They can be outlines showing the shapes of objects, or details and patterns. Lines can create edges, shapes, movement and they can create a sense of light and dark. They can be wiggly, curved, straight, zigzagged, broken or solid – and more! Grab a pencil and paper and give it a try – how many different lines can you draw? Sometimes, lines are used for shading or tones, with hatching or cross-hatching. Hatching is when parallel lines are drawn to show shadows and cross-hatching is when criss-crossed lines are used to do the same.

SHAPE

·······································

There are two types of shape in art: organic shapes and geometric shapes.
Organic shapes are natural and often irregular, and geometric shapes are precise and even.
Lines used to make geometric shapes, such as squares, rectangles and triangles, are straight,
but lines used to draw organic shapes, such as leaves and shells, are often more uneven, varied
and creative. Because they are natural rather than man-made, organic shapes are all slightly different.
Organic shapes can make a work of art or design seem more natural and real, while geometric shapes
look more designed and graphic. Which do you prefer?

TEXTURE

∙∙

Texture means how something feels, or looks as if it feels!
When you touch something, it might feel rough, smooth, sharp or soft – that's the texture.
In 3D art, artists create texture by using different materials and surfaces. When artists draw,
paint or print flat artworks, they can create illusions of texture using marks. For example, lines
can create the look of wood or bricks, while bright highlights can create the appearance
of smoothness and shine. Pick up some objects around you – how do they feel when you
touch them? Try drawing an everyday object and creating texture using marks.

SUBJECT

· ·

The subject matter of a work of art is what the piece is about. It's the topic.
For example, in a portrait of someone, the subject is that person. In a seascape, the subject
is the sea. Works of art sometimes contain symbols as well as subject matter. For example,
if there is a dog in a painting, the dog might symbolise faithfulness. In a painting with a landscape
at sunrise as its subject, the sunrise might symbolise hope. Not all artists include subjects in their
art – for instance, abstract art is often symbolic, rather than depicting a recognisable subject.

THEME

· ·

While the subject describes what we see, the theme is broader
and often about the artist's thoughts, feelings or ideas. Not all works of art have themes,
but if they do, they are usually suggested rather than obvious. The theme is often a hidden meaning.
An example of a subject and a theme in one artwork is a painting of a garden, with a theme of summer.
Common themes in art history include death, religion, love and nature. But it's up to you as an artist –
you're in charge of your subject and if you want to include a theme.

TONE

· ·

In art, tone describes lightness or darkness.
Because flat works of art are two-dimensional, many artists use different
tones – or shading – to create the illusion that things are solid and three-dimensional.
Different tones can also help to suggest depth and distance, to create an atmosphere and to show how
and where light falls on things. Depending on how strong the light is and where it falls, an object has
different tones in different places. All 3D things we see have many different tones and by creating
these in flat drawings or paintings, artists can make things look realistic and lifelike.

BRUSHWORK

· ·

The way a painter applies paint to surfaces with a brush is described as brushwork.
Because artists' brushes are made in different shapes, sizes and textures, artists can create various
effects with them, using different techniques. For example, broken brushwork – or using short dabs of
paint – can create paintings that look lively. Fluid brushwork means using long, smooth paint strokes with
fairly runny, thin paint, which can create a calm feeling. Invisible brushwork means that you can hardly
see the marks made by the artist's paintbrush! All of these different types of brushwork can change
the look of a painting.

CALLIGRAPHY

Calligraphy is what we call the art of producing decorative handwriting or lettering.
Calligraphy first became an important form of art in ancient China during the Shang dynasty,
closely followed by Japan and Islamic countries. It still remains an important form of art in many
of these countries today, and is now popular all around the world. Different countries have their own
methods, but most calligraphers use ink and a brush or pen to write their letters. Why don't you
give it a try – how many different styles can you use to write your own name or your
favourite word?

CARVING

Three-dimensional art is usually made using one of four methods: carving, modelling, casting or constructing. Since prehistoric times, sculptors have carved materials such as stone, wood, ivory or bone, using tools including chisels, hammers and mallets. We know this because some of the earliest known works of art are stone carvings, often of animals or human figures. Wood carving is another early form of art, but as wood often rots, there are few examples left! Many ancient Greek and Roman artists as well as artists of the Renaissance, such as Michelangelo, were skilful at carving huge sculptures out of marble.

SILHOUETTE

Named after Étienne de Silhouette, an 18th-century French minister
known for saving money, the phrase *à la Silhouette* grew to mean 'on the cheap'. His hobby was
cutting out paper portrait shapes, and a silhouette now describes a flat-looking outline of a person,
animal, object or scene in one plain colour. During the middle of the 18th century,
cutting out silhouette portraits from black card, usually in profile, became very popular
and skilled artists could look at a person, then cut out their silhouette in minutes. Plain, dark-coloured
silhouettes are usually placed on light-coloured backgrounds to make them stand out.

COLLAGE

A collage is a picture or pattern made up of all kinds of different materials,
glued to a surface. Collages have been made by professional artists since the early 20th century.
Pablo Picasso and Georges Braque, working in an art style we call Cubism, were the first to use collage
in their paintings. They cut up things like cardboard, newspaper and even old bus tickets
then glued them on their canvases. Collages are a great way to recycle old materials
and turn them into something new. See what you can find – you could
make a masterpiece from your recycling bin!

DRAWING

· ·

The word drawing can describe the drawing itself or the act of making a drawing.
Using mainly dry materials, such as pencils, crayons, charcoal and chalk, or thin, fluid materials such as ink, artists draw on many different surfaces, including paper, card and rock. Most drawings are flat and made up of lines, shapes and other marks. There are different types of drawing, such as lifelike, gestural, expressive, symbolic or abstract. Gestural and expressive drawings are usually made quickly, with vigorous marks. Lifelike drawings include perspective, textures and tone. Some drawings are even used as plans or preparation for paintings.

ENGRAVING

Engraving is a way of making prints by cutting a design or picture
into a metal plate. The picture or design is carved into the metal plate with
a steel engraving tool that looks like a fine chisel. Next, ink is rolled across the plate
and then wiped away, leaving ink only in the engraved areas. Then the plate is put into a press
with a damp sheet of paper placed against it. The inked lines are pressed against the paper,
leaving the back-to-front design. The engraved plate can be used
to print the design or picture again and again.

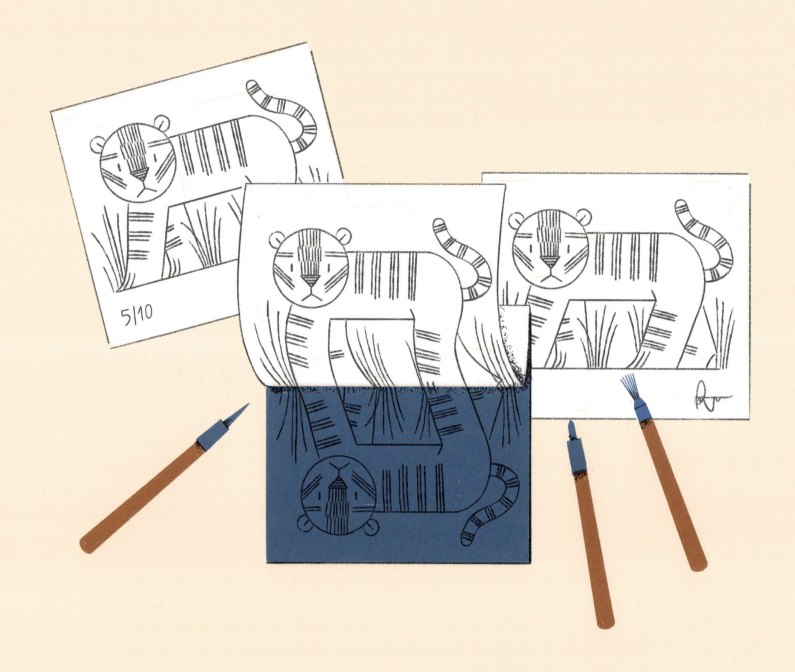

5/10

ETCHING

· ·

Etching is a form of printmaking. Artists begin by spreading a waxy substance
onto a metal plate, then a special needle is used to scratch a design through the wax coating onto
the metal below. The whole thing is dipped in acid, which makes deeper grooves in the scratched areas.
The artist then removes the wax, leaving the scratched design. To use the print, ink is rolled onto the
print so it sinks into the grooves. The plate is wiped, and a clean sheet of paper pressed onto it.
The ink-filled lines stick to the paper, creating the back-to-front design.

FORESHORTENING

Foreshortening is a form of dramatic perspective. When an object or a person is seen from a distance or from an unusual angle, they appear distorted. To see for yourself, stand in front of a mirror, hold out your arm and tilt up your hand so your palm is facing the mirror. Notice how large your hand appears compared to your body. This distortion is called foreshortening and artists paint and draw using it to create lifelike illusions. For example, if you draw people from a worm's eye view, their feet will be huge and their heads will be tiny.

FRESCO

A painting made on fresh plaster is known as a fresco.
The earliest frescoes were made in Greece in about 1600 BCE and
they were later made all over the world. Now we know them by their Italian name, fresco.
There are two types: buon (good) and secco (dry). In buon fresco, artists paint with pigment
on freshly applied damp plaster. The pigment sinks in and the painting becomes part of the wall
or ceiling. With fresco secco, the plaster is dry when artists paint on it,
and to make the paint stick, pigment is mixed with egg or glue.

GILDING

Gilding is a decorative method of coating an object with a thin layer of gold leaf, gold powder, silver or copper. Many different surfaces can be gilded, including metal, wood, porcelain and stone. Some of the earliest artists to use gilding were the ancient Egyptians – they often used it to decorate royal mummy cases and furniture. The ancient Greeks, Romans, medieval and Renaissance artists also gilded various objects. In the 18th-century Qing dynasty in China, gilding on porcelain was introduced and in the early 20th century, the Austrian artist Gustav Klimt added gilding to his paintings in his 'Golden Phase'.

GLASSBLOWING

Using a long tube, a furnace and a blob of softened glass, a glassblower can create beautiful glass objects such as vases, dishes and jugs. A glassblower begins by blowing through the tube, turning the blob into a bubble. Next, they twist, turn and swing the bubble skilfully over a hot furnace to soften it. Once the glass is in the glassblower's desired size and shape, it is left to cool for a few hours until it becomes hard. This method of glassblowing was invented by Syrian craftsmen in the 1st century BCE and it has hardly changed since then.

IMPASTO

· ·

For years, people thought that for a painting to show an artist's skill, the paint had to be thin with almost invisible brush marks. Then, in the 17th century, artists such as Rembrandt, Diego Velázquez and Peter Paul Rubens began applying thicker paint to their canvases. They also applied bright white highlights on top of their first layers. This technique is what we call impasto. By the late 19th century, more artists such as Vincent van Gogh painted with even thicker impasto and many artists followed the idea that thickly-textured impasto paint can be more expressive than flat, smooth paint.

PAINTING

From Monet to Picasso, da Vinci to van Gogh, many of the most popular artists are famous for their paintings. Using colours, tones, shapes, lines and textures, painters work with various paints such as oils, acrylics or watercolour. Most painters use brushes to apply their paints, while some use palette knives, rags or even their fingers. Oils and acrylics are often used on canvas or wood, while watercolour and gouache are generally used on thick paper. There are many reasons that artists paint, such as to express their feelings, or to paint something that pleases them, such as a flower.

PERSPECTIVE

· ·

To create the idea of three-dimensions on flat surfaces such as drawings or paintings,
many artists use a set of rules called perspective. Perspective creates illusions of distance and
depth, to make images more lifelike. There are two main kinds of perspective: linear and atmospheric.
Linear is about lines and atmospheric is about light. With linear perspective, objects that are further
away are smaller than objects that are close up – lines that go away from us appear to become
closer together. In atmospheric, or aerial perspective, things in the distance become less
detailed and appear bluer and a bit hazy.

PHOTOGRAPHY

· ·

The word photography comes from two ancient Greek words: *photo* meaning 'light',
and *graph* meaning 'drawing'. So photography really means drawing with light! A photograph
is an image made by a chemical reaction which records the impression of light on a light-sensitive
material. Early photographs were called sun pictures, because sunlight was used to create them.
Today, a camera uses a lens to focus light onto a light-sensitive surface. The invention of the
camera created a big change in the art world – a realistic image that would take ages to
draw could be recorded within a fraction of a second.

POINTILLISM

··

At the end of the 19th century, an artist called Georges Seurat invented a method
of painting that we now call Pointillism, although he called it Divisionism. Some artists he knew,
known as the Impressionists, broke traditions of painting by using small dabs of colour, but Seurat
and another artist, Paul Signac, went further, painting only small dots of pure colour to create whole
paintings. Georges Seurat believed that rather than mixing the colours on his palette, by putting
dots of pure colour side by side on his canvases, from a distance, the colours appear to
be brighter and blended.

SCREENPRINT

To make a screenprint, artists make stencils of their designs,
put them on a mesh screen, then place that on a sheet of paper. Thick ink is applied
with a tool called a 'squeegee' that is dragged across the screen. The squeegee forces the ink
through the mesh, but not through the stencils, so the ink that sticks to the paper underneath
covers everything except the stencilled areas. To add more colours and shapes, the screen is
washed and new stencils are added. The dried first print is put underneath
and a different coloured ink is spread across the top.

PRINTMAKING

· ·

Printmaking is a method artists use to make copies of a single image. There are various different methods of printmaking, and most involve ink being moved from one surface to another. Some of the most popular printmaking techniques include woodcutting, etching, lithography, screen-printing, lino cutting, collagraphy, engraving, aquatinting and mono-printing. In all types of printmaking, artists create images using a material such as wood or a metal plate, or even stencils, then add ink, paint or dye and transfer their designs on to another surface, such as paper or fabric. In all printmaking, the design comes out back to front.

RELIEF

· ·

An image or design that is raised from its base, like a 3D picture or pattern, is called a relief. Reliefs are almost a cross between a 2D image and a work of sculpture. When a relief is raised only slightly from its base, it's called a low or bas-relief. Reliefs that stick out quite far from their backgrounds are described as high relief. And middle reliefs are somewhere in between low and high! Some artists mix low, middle and high relief all in one artwork to create perspective or to show that some things are further in the distance.

CERAMICS

··

While pottery objects are always made with clay, ceramics can be made of clay or other materials, such as porcelain or brick. Ceramics include things like tiles, plates, vases, sinks and jugs. Ceramic materials are soft at first and the artist – or ceramicist – shapes them into objects, then puts them in a special hot oven called a kiln where they are fired – or baked. After the firing process, these objects are hard, heatproof and easily broken. The artist can then paint their ceramics by brushing them with special glazes that create wonderful colours, patterns and effects, with a beautiful shine.

SCULPTURE

Three-dimensional art is known as sculpture and artists have been creating sculptures
for thousands of years. One of the earliest we know about was created in about 35,000 BCE.
Sculptures can be made of many different materials, such as clay, wax, stone, metal, glass, wood and
plaster. A variety of techniques are used to create sculptures, including carving, modelling, moulding,
casting and welding. Before the 20th century, traditional methods and materials were used
and sculptures usually imitated things from real life. But from the early 20th century,
sculpture began changing and abstract creations have been made, often with unusual materials.

POTTERY

When damp clay is shaped and fired – or baked – at a high temperature, it hardens.
This is called pottery, a type of ceramic. Items created in this way are called pottery and the place
where they are made also has the same name – a pottery. There are three types: earthenware, stoneware
and porcelain. Earthenware is cheapest, made from a lower quality clay. Stoneware is longer-lasting and
more expensive, and porcelain is the most expensive, made from the highest quality clay.
Potters shape clay with tools, their hands or with a machine called a potter's wheel
which helps create round objects.

STENCIL

· ·

As with screen-printing, etching, engraving and printmaking, stencils allow artists to repeat identical patterns. Usually made of paper, plastic, card or metal, stencils have designs cut out of them. Artists place stencils on to a surface, such as a sheet of paper, a piece of fabric or even a wall, and draw, colour or paint with sponges, spray paint, paint brushes or special stencil brushes inside the shapes. The colour goes through the cut-out areas only, as the stencil covers the blank areas, leaving the design on the surface underneath. Some designers use stencils to decorate furniture, curtains or clothing.

WASH

·····································

In painting, a wash creates a gentle, blended colour, with no visible lines of the brushstrokes used to create it. Using a large, damp paintbrush soaked in watery paint or ink, an artist uses smooth, long strokes on to a wet or dry surface such as paper, card or canvas, so the wash creates a transparent layer of colour. A graduated wash smoothly changes from dark to light, light to dark, or between different colours. Why don't you give it a try – a wash could be a great technique for painting something like the sky, a sunset or the sea.

WOODCUT

· ·

One of the oldest forms of printmaking, a woodcut is made by an artist drawing his or her design on to a wooden surface. Then, using small, sharp cutting tools, the artist gouges around the design, removing the areas of wood that won't be printed. Once cut away, the wood can't be put back, so mistakes can't be made! Ink is then applied to the wood with a small roller, and the artist presses the wood on to fabric or paper to print the pattern. To create coloured woodcuts, the artist has to create separate wooden blocks for each colour.

ABSTRACT

Any designs, patterns or marks that do not represent things from the world around us can be called abstract. Abstract art can be made with any materials, be 2D or 3D, and can be a great way for artists to express their feelings and creativity. Some artworks are partly abstract, representing things from the everyday world but in a distorted way. Artists have been making abstract images for thousands of years, but it was not until the early 20th century that we began to call these abstract. Jackson Pollock, Piet Mondrian and Wassily Kandinsky are examples of famous abstract artists.

ANCIENT EGYPTIAN

Much of our knowledge of the ancient Egyptians comes from their art.
From the many works of art they created, we can learn about what they looked like, wore,
did, and what they considered to be important. Most of the art was made to help rich people reach
the afterlife after they had died. Because Ancient Egyptian art often included religious themes, artists
followed strict rules about drawing, painting and sculpting. Ancient Egyptian art therefore changed
little over 3,000 years. The art included statues, wall paintings and paintings on papyrus.
Even their picture writing, or hieroglyphs, was an art form.

ANCIENT GREEK

From around 800 BCE to 146 BCE, the ancient Greek people lived and produced
their pioneering art. This art is usually divided into four periods: Geometric, Archaic, Classical
and Hellenistic. Each period had different styles, but all their art aimed to show perfection, avoiding
any imperfections they saw in the real world. Ancient Greek artists created paintings, sculptures
and pottery, particularly their black and red decorated pots, which were also practical objects
as well as works of art. Early pottery had black figures on red backgrounds, but after
the 5th century BCE, they changed to red figures on black backgrounds.

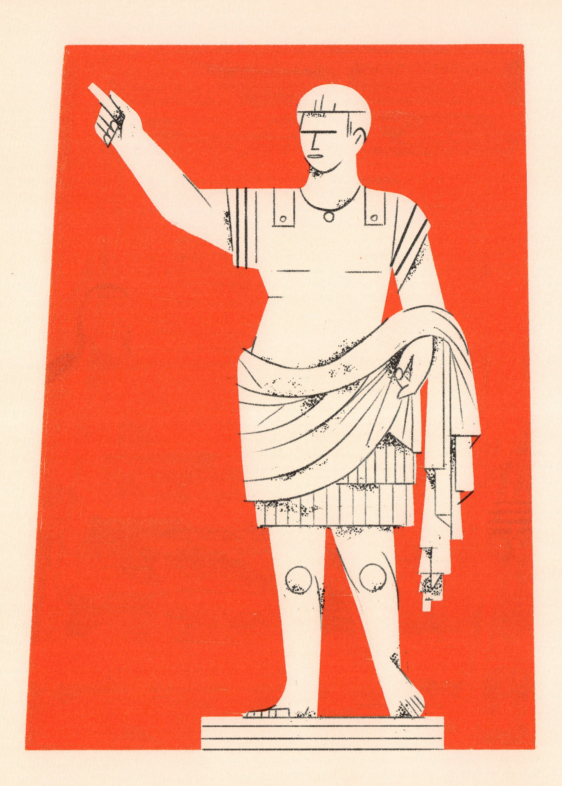

ANCIENT ROMAN

· ·

From about 753 BCE to 476 BCE, the ancient Romans ruled much of Europe.
Roman artists admired the art of the ancient Greeks, and copied their style, or Greek artists
worked for them, often creating art for the wealthy and powerful to celebrate their achievements.
Sculptures were often displayed to be seen and admired, placed in parks and public buildings. These could
be statues of people or gods, busts (sculptures of a person's head and shoulders) or reliefs on walls.
They were often very grand and impressive. Artists also painted on walls and used encaustic
(wax painting) on sarcophagi (coffins).

BAROQUE

· ·

From about 1575 to about 1770, a new style of art started in Italy which soon
spread across Europe. This style was what we now call Baroque art. The Baroque style began
when Catholic Church leaders asked artists to make paintings more emotional and dramatic, to glorify
Catholicism. So much Baroque art tells stories from the Bible, making them extra vivid. Baroque
paintings and sculpture are usually dramatic, with spectacular lighting and a sense of movement.
Baroque sculpture was often made to be viewed from different angles. Baroque artists
include Diego Velázquez, Rembrandt, Gian Lorenzo Bernini and Peter Paul Rubens.

CUBISM

....

From about 1907, artists began developing a new style of painting. Rather than depicting images from one viewpoint, trying to pretend that flat surfaces are three-dimensional, they began painting things from several angles at once, to show as much of their subjects as they could using two dimensions. Because their art ended up looking like geometric shapes, it became nicknamed Cubism. Picasso and Georges Braque were the first two artists to develop Cubism and from 1912, they began adding collage to their paintings to show even more reality. Their ideas changed how art developed, a major moment in art history.

EXPRESSIONISM

· ·

Soon after the horrors of the First World War, starting in Germany,
some artists began creating art that expressed their emotions, such as anger, fear, sorrow
or happiness, rather than trying to copy the reality of things. Although some artists before them
had also expressed their feelings in their art, for example, van Gogh, this was the first time that
several artists did it at the same time and their art became called Expressionism. Every Expressionist
had an individual way of 'expressing' his or her emotions, such as distorting or exaggerating shapes
or colours. Not much looked natural or realistic.

FAUVISM

· ·

In 1905, an art critic at an exhibition was shocked at the bold brushstrokes, vibrant colours and distortions of some artists' paintings. He nicknamed them *Les Fauves* – French for 'The Wild Beasts'. The artists included Henri Matisse and André Derain who had been inspired when painting in the South of France that summer. Their paintings were almost abstract, made using simple shapes, unnatural colours, loosely applied paint and often complementary colours to make their paintings look brighter. They were inspired by artists including van Gogh and Seurat. Although their ideas continued, the Fauvists were only together from 1905 to 1907.

FUTURISM

··

With many new inventions, life in the early 20th century was very exciting. In Italy, some young artists wanted to break with the past and look to the future instead. They called their movement Futurism, and created art that included machines, speed and movement. They wanted libraries and museums to close because these focus on the past, and instead thought that war would clear the way for the future. Artists including Umberto Boccioni, Carlo Carrà, Luigi Russolo, Giacomo Balla and Gino Severini created art that expressed change and motion, depicting things like speeding cars, trains, cyclists, dancers, runners and animals.

IMPRESSIONISM

· ·

In France in the late 19th century, some artists began painting in the open air, often completing their work there rather than back in the studio. This new style of painting captured passing moments but critics weren't sure about it – they thought the paintings were just 'impressions', not the usual neat, detailed paintings finished in the studio. The Impressionists continued to paint fleeting moments, capturing atmosphere, focusing on light, colour and weather effects, using small, quick brush marks and bright colours. Some of the main Impressionists were Claude Monet, Berthe Morisot, Camille Pissarro, Alfred Sisley, Auguste Renoir and Mary Cassatt.

MODERNISM

· ·

At the start of the 20th century, several artists, architects, writers, designers and musicians decided that new inventions in science and technology could change the world for the better and began thinking about new ideas. The artists rejected traditional approaches to art, and began working in different styles, mainly abandoning realistic representations of things that had been so important in art of the past. They experimented with different materials, techniques and methods as well as line, form and colour. There was no one set style, but Modernism included Impressionism, Post-Impressionism, Cubism, Futurism, Expressionism, Suprematism, Constructivism, De Stijl and Abstract Expressionism.

NEOCLASSICISM

A new style of art developed in the late 18th century that became called Neoclassicism. Reacting to the drama of Baroque art, it came after the discovery of the ancient Roman ruins of Pompeii and Herculaneum, and the publication of *A History of Ancient Art* in 1764. The discoveries sparked a widespread craze for the art, architecture and design of ancient Greece and Rome. Artists produced paintings and sculpture that followed some ideas of the ancient Greeks and Romans, with clean, straight lines, smooth paint or carving and plain colours. Neoclassical artists included Jean Auguste Dominique Ingres and Antonio Canova.

POP ART

Pop art began in the mid-1950s in Britain and in the early 1960s in America, with a group of artists who rebelled against what they saw as the snobbishness of art. They believed that what was exhibited in galleries did not reflect normal people's lives. So they created images based on things everyone would recognise, including films, celebrities, advertising, packaging, pop music, magazines, newspapers, comics and mass-produced products such as soup cans and soft drinks. Many Pop artists, including Andy Warhol and Roy Lichtenstein, worked with materials and methods from advertising and commercial printing to reflect the modern consumer society.

POST-IMPRESSIONISM

. . . .

The term Post-Impressionism was first used by the artist and art critic Roger Fry for an exhibition held in London in 1910, called 'Manet and the Post-Impressionists'. By then, all the artists featured in his exhibition had died. 'Post' means 'after' in Latin, and the artists he called Post-Impressionists included Vincent van Gogh, Paul Cézanne, Paul Gauguin, Henri de Toulouse-Lautrec and Georges Seurat. They did not work together and each artist had their own ideas, but they all followed on from Impressionism. They also all represented subjects from real life, often distorting them slightly, using vivid colours and distinctive brushwork.

REALISM

Beginning in France in about 1840, starting with Gustave Courbet, some artists and writers moved away from the idealism and exaggerations of Romanticism. Instead they chose to represent down-to-earth, everyday life. Without adding any emotional interpretations as Romanticism had done, they depicted everyday subjects and people. Much of their subject matter included peasants and working-class people going about their ordinary daily lives, rather than the rich and powerful people of society, or important stories that had previously dominated art. This subject matter, all painted or sculpted to look natural, shocked many people, as it seemed to criticise the upper classes.

RENAISSANCE

· ·

The term Renaissance (French for 'rebirth') describes developments in art, science, architecture and writing that occurred in Italy from about 1400, after classical art and writing had been rediscovered. While many Renaissance artists still created religious subjects, they also depicted Greek and Roman mythology and lifelike portraits. Renaissance art is described as: Early Renaissance, which included artists such as Giotto, Masaccio, Botticelli and Donatello; High Renaissance, which became even more realistic, with artists including Michelangelo, da Vinci and Raphael; and the Northern Renaissance that occurred in Europe, north of the Alps, including Pieter Bruegel, Jan van Eyck and Hieronymus Bosch.

ROMANTICISM

From the end of the 1700s to the 1800s, some writers, musicians and artists reacted to things that were happening around the world, including the Industrial, American and French Revolutions. The artists began creating a new style of art, expressing feelings, drama and the power of nature. Romantic art expressed spirituality, the imagination and mystery. Subject matter included landscapes, religion, revolutions, history and portraits. Some Romantic painters believed that images of nature could affect people's moods, so they created calm or atmospheric scenes. Some famous Romantic artists include John Constable, Caspar David Friedrich, Eugene Delacroix, William Turner and Francisco Goya.

SURREALISM

· ·

Art that explores our unconscious thoughts and feelings is called Surrealism. The movement started in 1924 in France. It first emerged in writing, but with the goal of expressing the subconscious, delving into dreams and emotions, Surrealism was also perfectly suited for visual art. Some of the most famous Surrealist artists included Jean Arp, Max Ernst, André Masson, Joan Miró, Salvador Dalí, Belgian René Magritte, Paul Nash and Dorothea Tanning. They created all kinds of art, often including unexpected objects appearing together in dreamlike paintings and sculptures and 'automatism', which was a method of drawing and painting, without consciously thinking.

SYMBOLISM

Unlike Impressionism, where artists painted what they saw, Symbolist art suggested ideas through symbols. Starting in the late 19th century with French, Russian and Belgian artists, Symbolists created art that expressed ideas beyond reality, often suggesting spiritual meanings and explaining things like dreams, visions and death. So even though many Symbolist artists showed realistic-looking things from the real world, their art usually represented something more, or something completely different. Symbolists did not use the traditional symbols that we usually see in many works of art, but created signs that were personal to the artists and not always clear to viewers.

ANIMATION

Animators make things look as if they are moving. The earliest animators drew collections of pictures, each slightly different so that when filmed one after the other, they appeared to move. Some animators use the same technique, but use models and take a series of photographs of them. Today, many animations are created with computer graphics. To make your own animation without technology, draw an object or character on all pages of a small notepad. On each page, draw the object in a slightly different place. When the notepad is flipped through at speed, page by page, the animation moves!

CARTOON

Since the 1840s, the word 'cartoon' has been used to describe simplified drawings often created to make people laugh. Cartoons appear in newspapers, books, magazines and on TV. Some cartoons are made for children and some are for adults. Comic strips are types of cartoon. Some of the earliest cartoon characters are animals including Daffy Duck, Bugs Bunny, Mickey Mouse and Donald Duck, but the first cartoons, made hundreds of years ago, were large plans of tapestries, paintings or mosaics. Artists pierced holes in the cartoons and dabbed charcoal powder over the holes to mark the shapes on other surfaces.

CONCEPTUAL

Another word for concept is idea, and in Conceptual art, the artwork is all about the artist's idea, more than how it looks. Although some artists, particularly Marcel Duchamp, started making art focusing on ideas in the early 20th century, the Conceptualism movement began in the mid-1960s. From that time, artists around the world have created Conceptual art. These artists do not make paintings or sculptures – they express their ideas with often unexpected materials, such as the lights, springs and shadows in the image above. Some of the most influential Conceptual artists include Joseph Beuys, Sol LeWitt and Jenny Holzer.

GRAFFITI

Bold images or words, usually made in public places, are called graffiti.
The earliest graffiti was made a long time ago, in places like ancient Rome, by people using knives to carve words and drawings on stone walls or columns. Today, graffiti artists use materials like spray paints and marker pens. There are different types of graffiti – some is made as a political protest, some is detailed, decorative or artistic and some is simple – a single word or person's name.
Street art is usually painted with permission but graffiti is often illegal.
Banksy is a famous – but anonymous – graffiti artist.

GRAPHICS

All art that is produced on flat surfaces, such as drawing, painting, printmaking, computer art, lettering and calligraphy is known as graphic art or graphics. Graphic art is visual information, made to communicate ideas clearly, usually with pictures, designs and words. Graphic designers used to be called commercial artists, because graphic art is generally created for commercial use, such as advertising, packaging or for film or TV credits. Graphics can be seen in such things as magazines, books, online, computer games, manuals, leaflets and posters. If you were to create some graphic art to advertise something what would you choose?

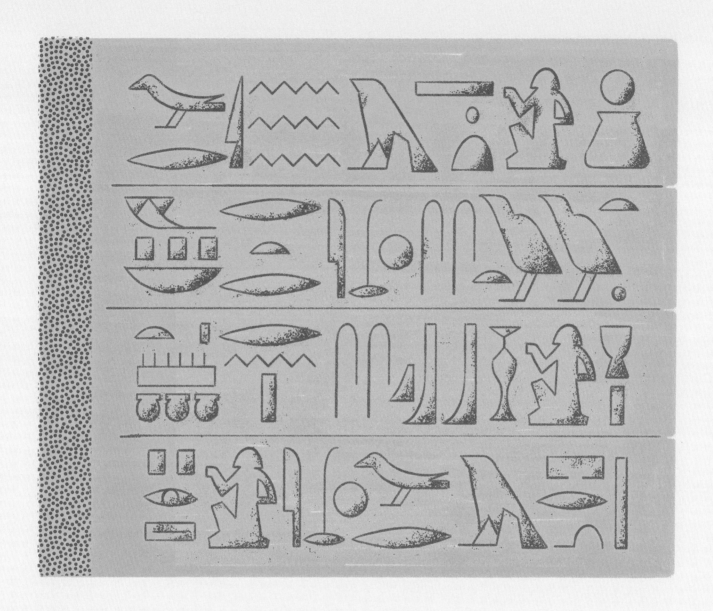

HIEROGLYPHS

· ·

Some ancient writing systems that use pictures and symbols instead of letters and words are called hieroglyphics, and each symbol is called a hieroglyph. The word comes from a Greek word meaning 'sacred carving'. Several ancient societies, such as the Mayans, made hieroglyphs, but the most famous were made by the ancient Egyptians. Ancient Egyptian scribes carved or painted their hieroglyphs on tomb walls, temple columns, clay tablets and papyrus scrolls. There are more than 700 ancient Egyptian hieroglyphs, each representing different sounds or words, or objects such as the sun or animals. Why not create some of your own!

ILLUSION

· ·

An illusion is something that is not what it first appears to be.
Many artists create illusions by making viewers think that the art they are looking at
is real: these are optical illusions. The word 'optical' relates to how we see, and artists use shapes,
colours, light, lines and patterns to create illusions that fool our eyes. Illusions of real objects
or scenes can be made with certain painting techniques, and illusions of movement
can be made with lines placed different distances apart. For example, Bridget Riley
created lines and shapes in black and white that appear to move.

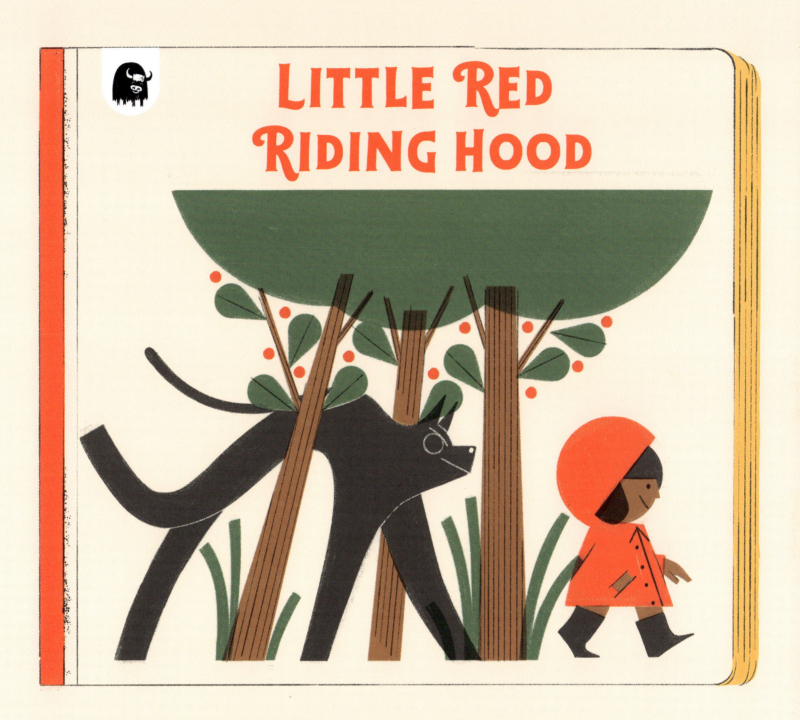

ILLUSTRATION

Images that communicate messages or ideas are called illustrations.
Usually, illustrations help to tell stories, explain or decorate the words in books, newspapers, magazines, advertising, posters, leaflets, manuals, packaging or online. They can be simple diagrams or detailed scenes, in colour or in black and white, big or small and nearly always flat (2D). Illustrations can be created in many different materials and styles. Illustrators often specialise in particular areas of illustration, such as technical or scientific, fashion design or children's books. Have a go at illustrating one of your favourite stories, or invent a new one of your own!

INSTALLATION

An installation is a style of usually large, three-dimensional art that uses many different materials. Although some earlier artists produced large 3D works of art, they were not called installations until the 1970s. Installations are made by artists to change the way spaces appear. They can be permanent or temporary and are usually displayed in museums, galleries or public spaces. The materials used to create installations can be varied and are often made of materials that have not been used traditionally for art. Many are 'site-specific' which means that they are designed especially for the places where they are exhibited.

KINETIC

In the early 20th century, some artists began creating artworks that actually moved. These artworks are called kinetic, from the Greek word *kinesis* meaning 'movement'. Through their art, kinetic artists often aim to explore movement, to introduce ideas about time, to show the importance of machines and technology in the modern world and to explore how we see things. To create actual movement in their art, some artists use machines, while others create pieces that move because of the natural movement of air around them. Kinetic artist Alexander Calder achieved this in his mobiles which moved when the wind blew.

LAND ART

Land art is when an artist turns a natural landscape into art. Also called earth and environmental art, land art is usually made using local, natural materials such as ice, rocks or twigs. It is often temporary and involves some form of sculpture or structure. This means that it is affected by the environment, such as the weather, and is natural, organic and ever-changing. Many land artists take photographs of their work before it decays or disappears. A fun way to try land art is by using fallen leaves to create patterns on the ground in your garden or park.

MINIATURE

You might have seen a big masterpiece in a gallery or museum, but have you ever seen a mini one?
During the 1520s, miniature portraits became popular and were often worn in lockets and brooches.
Miniature painting is also called 'limning', and the artists who produce them work with tiny brushes,
making fine marks on card, copper, ivory or vellum (fine parchment made from calfskin). There is no
set size for an artwork to be described as miniature, but it can usually fit inside the palm of a hand.
Why not give it a try and create a mini self-portrait!

MOSAIC

. . . .

Pictures or decorations made with small pieces of stone, glass, shells or tiles are called mosaics.
They have been made for thousands of years by, among others, ancient Greeks and Romans and the
Byzantines. Mosaics can be created indoors or outdoors on walls, floors and ceilings. The ancient Romans
called mosaics *tesserae*, which means 'cubes' and their mosaics tell us about who the Romans were, what
they valued and what their life was like. In the medieval period, mosaics were used to decorate churches.
Mosaic artists create designs, then put the small pieces in place and set them in cement.

MURAL

A mural is a large painting on a wall or ceiling. Many murals are so large that they seem to change the space around them. In ancient Roman buildings, walls and ceilings were often painted with murals. They became even more lifelike during the Renaissance and the Baroque period. Over time, murals have been painted on the inside and outside walls of many public buildings, such as palaces, temples, tombs and museums. Artists who paint murals have worked with many techniques, including encaustic (also known as 'hot wax painting'), tempera (pigment mixed with egg), in fresco and with oil paints.

TESSELLATION

· ·

Patterns of interlocking shapes are called tessellations. These are shapes that fit together, are the same or similar, and are arranged across a surface without overlaps or gaps. They fit closely together like pieces of a jigsaw and have been created since ancient times. The Latin word *tessella* means 'a small piece of clay', stone or glass that is used to make mosaics, but all sorts of tessellations have been created, from ancient architecture to modern art. For instance, tiles on walls or floors and patchwork quilts are tessellated, while detailed tessellations were made by the artist M. C. Escher.

PERFORMANCE

Art performed by an artist for an audience is called performance art. It can be planned or spontaneous and can be filmed or repeated in different places. Often made by artists using their own bodies, the physical movement is a change from traditional art forms such as painting and sculpture. Costumes and props can be used to help show the artist's ideas. Performance art can be many things, but it is often unexpected and unusual, and makes people think. Marina Abramović is a performance artist known for testing how she thinks and feels – and testing those who watch her performances.

PORTRAIT

· ·

A painting or photograph of someone, often of the head and shoulders, is called a portrait. A self-portrait is a portrait that an artist produces of themselves. Before the invention of photography, portraits were the only way to record someone's appearance. Many have been created to show a person's importance, beauty, wealth or intelligence. Some portraits are not always an accurate image of the person – Henry VIII chose his fourth wife, Anne of Cleves, from her portrait but he was disappointed with how she looked in real life! The ancient Greeks and Romans created portraits on their coins and medals.

PREHISTORIC

Humans have made art for thousands of years. Prehistoric means 'before history' and it refers to a time before people made written records. People created art before they invented writing, so prehistoric art tells us about those who made it and what life was like for them. Some of the earliest prehistoric artworks ever found are tiny carved sculptures of women, made about 35,000 years ago. Soon after, artists created paintings, carvings and drawings on rocks and in caves, mainly of animals, in countries including Spain, France, Indonesia, the USA and Australia. Prehistoric art is sometimes still discovered even now!

PRIMITIVISM

In the 1890s, Paul Gauguin moved to Tahiti and began producing brightly coloured, simplified paintings. In 1906, Picasso took inspiration from African tribal masks and used some of the ideas he saw in them in his own art. The term Primitivism began to be used by European artists to describe this fascination that grew with what was then called primitive art. 'Primitive' art included tribal art from Africa, the South Pacific and Indonesia, and prehistoric and European folk art. Other artists, including Matisse, Picasso, Derain and Braque, began producing art with simplified shapes and unnatural colours based on this influence.

SCAPE

· ·

The word 'scape' describes a scene, usually a painting or a photograph.
Views of towns are called townscapes; views of cities are known as cityscapes
and ocean views are seascapes. Scenes or scapes of the natural world are known as landscapes
and have been popular among artists across the world for centuries. Landscapes can include hills,
rivers, trees, mountains, lakes and skies. Many artists depict what they see in their scapes,
while some capture a mood or an atmosphere, or suggest something mystical. Some artists
imagine their own scapes, while others like to recreate real views that they have seen.

STILL LIFE

· ·

Drawings, paintings and prints of anything that does not move, such as food, flowers, toys or books, is called still life. Still life can include manmade or natural objects, and artists who depict the objects usually group them together to explore details like colour, shape or texture, or sometimes to symbolise more abstract ideas. For instance, an egg might represent new life. Create your own still life drawing or painting! Gather some interesting objects, arrange them on a table and start sketching. Really look closely at the objects and the shapes between them. Include as much detail as you can.

TEXTILES

· ·

Textile art is one of the oldest forms of art. Any cloth, fabric or material that is woven, knitted or felted is a textile. Most textiles are made from a single, fine structure called a 'fibre'. Fibres can be natural or synthetic. Textiles were made by hand or with simple machines until the 18th century but today, most textiles are made by big, special machines in factories. Artists use textiles in different ways – they might print on them using batik, weave them, design and paint patterns on them, or embroider them. Textiles can also be made into clothes and costumes.

AUCTION

· ·

Auctions are public sales where people bid for things. The person who offers the highest bid buys the item for sale. Unlike shops, auction houses do not have cash desks or set prices on the things for sale. Normally, an auction catalogue is produced that lists the items for sale. People at an art auction (or online viewers) who want to buy any of the artworks on sale, offer a price and each bid is higher than the last. There are lots of auction houses around the world and people sometimes bid very high prices for work by famous artists.

EXHIBITION

An art exhibition is where artworks are shown to the public. Usually, exhibitions are temporary and are held in halls, shops, galleries, museums, libraries and other large public spaces. Some exhibitions cost money to enter, some are free, some show artworks of a common subject or idea, some feature work by a single artist, some display art by certain groups of artists, such as the Cubists, and others might showcase a specific type of art, such as paintings. Whatever the theme, exhibitions are great places for artists to show their work and for viewers to see real art in close-up.

GALLERY

· ·

An art gallery or museum is a building or space where works of art are displayed,
often for a longer time than in an exhibition. Paintings are the most commonly displayed works of
art, but sculpture, textiles, costumes, photographs, collages, prints and installations are also shown.
Sometimes galleries also show performance art or hold temporary exhibitions. Some galleries contain
works of art by specific artists, some specialise in particular types of art and some focus on certain
time periods. Some famous galleries around the world include the Louvre in Paris,
Tate Modern in London and the Metropolitan in New York.

SPATIAL DESIGN

Spatial design is a type of art that blends architecture, interior design, landscape architecture and landscape design. Spatial designers think about how people use buildings or spaces and the way those people feel when they use them. They usually aim to design spaces so that they are enjoyable for the people who use them, but also to make people feel happier and healthier. Like other designers, spatial designers consider colour and materials, but they also consider things like flow, harmony, balance, light and where things are placed. They then work with architects and builders to bring their designs to life.

STUDIO

· ·

An art studio is an artist's workroom. It is where artists plan, experiment and create their art. A studio is a place where an artist can focus and be creative, surrounded by his or her own materials. Shared studios can be a great way for artists to interact with other artists and discuss ideas with each other. Many artists prefer their studios to face north, because north light does not change throughout the day as much as southern light. If you had your own art studio, where would it be? What would it look like? How big would it be?

WORKSHOP

· ·

During the 14th to 19th centuries in Europe, the most common way to become an artist was to join an artist's workshop as an apprentice. Many Renaissance artists had workshops where they trained apprentices and worked with assistants who learned their craft over several years. Some paintings made by assistants in workshops are signed 'from the workshop of…' with the name of the artist who owned the workshop. Today, most new artists no longer learn this way but workshops are still part of the art world – they are busy, creative shared places with tools, materials and space for experimenting.

AUTHOR'S NOTE

Art is amazing – it can dazzle us with its beauty, astound us with its skills and puzzle us with its ideas. It can be breathtaking, funny, shocking and astonishing. Art has been made by so many people for so many years, that it can also be mind-boggling! And we're still making art now. This will become part of art history, and children in the future will marvel over it, just as we do about ancient art. I hope you find these 100 topics as interesting to read about as I found them to write.

Art has always fascinated me – I never get bored writing about it or making it, and I really hope you feel the same. What facts did you find the most interesting? What surprised you? What inspired you? I'm always finding out new things about art, and if, like me, this book makes you want to find out even more, check out the next few pages for information about art galleries, museums, books and online resources.

Happy reading – and making!

Susie Hodge

GALLERIES

There are so many art galleries and museums around the world. Here's a list of some of the most popular, home to some of the most famous paintings ever created:

UK
Ashmolean Museum of Art
Oxford, UK

The National Gallery
London, UK

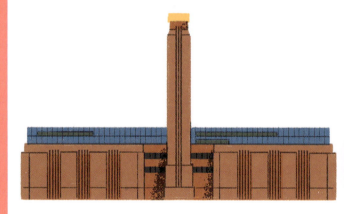

Tate Modern
London, UK

Whitworth Art Gallery
Manchester, UK

Walker Art Gallery
Liverpool, UK

ITALY
Uffizi Gallery
Florence, Italy

Galleria Borghese
Rome, Italy

Vatican Museums
Rome, Italy

AND MUSEUMS

SPAIN

The Guggenheim Museum
Bilbao, Spain

Museo del Prado
Madrid, Spain

AUSTRIA

Kunsthistorisches Museum
Vienna, Austria

RUSSIA

Pushkin Museum of Fine Arts
Moscow, Russia

The Hermitage Museum
St Petersburg, Russia

GERMANY

Gemäldegalerie Alte Meister
Dresden, Germany

Alte Pinakothek
Munich, Germany

Neue Pinakothek
Munich, Germany

THE NETHERLANDS

The Rijksmuseum
Amsterdam, The Netherlands

Mauritshuis
The Hague, The Netherlands

DENMARK

The Ny Carlsberg Glyptotek
Copenhagen, Denmark

FRANCE

Musée du Louvre
Paris, France

Musée d'Orsay
Paris, France

Centre Pompidou
Paris, France

JAPAN

Bridgestone Museum of Art
Tokyo, Japan

AUSTRALIA

National Gallery of Australia
Canberra, Australia

USA

The Art Institute of Chicago
Illinois, USA

National Gallery of Art
Washington D.C., USA

Guggenheim
New York, USA

Metropolitan Museum of Art
New York, USA

Museum of Fine Arts in Boston
Massachusetts, USA

TIMELINE: THE HISTORY OF ART

Around 30,000-4000 BCE
Prehistoric art – the earliest art we know of. Included stone and bone statues and cave and rock paintings.

Around 3500-539 BCE
The art of Mesopotamia, from the region known today as Iraq, included story-telling reliefs and sculptures.

Around 3100 BCE-395 CE
For about 3,000 years, ancient Egyptian artists created reliefs, wall paintings, sculptures and paintings on papyrus.

Around 2000-1500 BCE
On the island of Crete, the Minoan civilisation developed. They made pottery, sculptures and wall paintings.

Around 1650-400 BCE
The Mycenaean civilisation developed on mainland Greece. Their art was similar to the Minoans, but more relaxed.

Around 1450 BCE-220 CE
Chinese art remained the same for almost 4,000 years. Artists were inspired by the natural world and often painted on silk or parchment.

Around 700-31 BCE
Ancient Greek art developed over hundreds of years. Artists created perfect-looking figure sculptures, pottery and panel paintings. They painted their sculptures in bright colours that has since worn off.

202 BCE-200 CE
Ancient Roman artists followed the ancient Greeks, but made their art a bit less 'perfect' and more natural. They made pottery, sculptures, reliefs, wall paintings and mosaics.

313-843
Early Christian art started in the city of Byzantium (now Istanbul) and included mosaics, murals, illuminations (decorated manuscripts) and reliefs.

661-1923
Islamic art rarely includes people, it mainly involves patterns and lettering, including calligraphy and wall decorations.

500-1453
Medieval and Byzantine art was all about Christianity. Medieval art was made in Christian Europe, and Byzantine art was made by the Greek-speaking Byzantine Empire, mainly in Constantinople, and included frescos and mosaics.

1122-1350
Gothic art in Europe was religious and included stained glass, panel paintings and illuminations.

1255-1350
Mainly in Italy, the art made at this time by artists including Cimabue, Giotto and Simone Martini, is often called Pre-Renaissance.

1420-1530
The Renaissance was a time when artists experimented with realistic styles more than any had done since the ancient Greeks and Romans.

1530-1610
Mannerism, mainly in Spain and Italy, included El Greco, Parmigianino and Tintoretto.

1600-1750
Baroque art is dramatic, with strong light effects and compositions. Artists include Rembrandt, Velázquez, Peter Paul Rubens, Caravaggio, Artemisia and Gentileschi.

1615-1868
Ukiyo-e art in Japan means 'pictures of the floating world'. These were mainly colourful woodblock prints made during the Edo period and depicted everyday scenes in Japan.

1700-1770
Rococo art and design was decorative and happy, with paintings and sculpture often showing people enjoying themselves. Rococo artists included Jean-Antoine Watteau, Canaletto, Jean-Honoré Fragonard and François Boucher.

1750-1850
Neoclassical art followed ideas of ancient Greek and Roman artists, with the artists creating grand paintings and sculpture.

1780-1850
Romanticism developed in art and writing through new interests in nature and in expressing personal feelings. Artists included John Constable, J.M.W. Turner, William Blake, Caspar David Friedrich, Eugène Delacroix and Henry Fuseli.

Around 1840-1900
Realism began when some artists and writers chose to represent everyday life and ordinary people rather than the rich and powerful who were usually shown in art.

1860-1900
Impressionism began in France, when some artists began painting in the open air rather than in the studio. Artists captured passing moments, light, colour and weather effects in bright colours.

1880-1906
Post-Impressionism was an art movement where the artists involved had different goals. They were not a group, although most of them were French and their art included bright colours in their paintings.

1905-1907
Fauvism was a French art movement, including Matisse, Derain, Raoul Dufy, Georges Rouault and Maurice de Vlaminck. They painted with bold colours, distorted shapes and loose brushstrokes.

1905-1940s
Expressionism showed the artist's inner feelings or ideas rather than real life, usually painted in unnatural colours with free brushwork. It began in Germany, with small groups of artists working together.

1909-1914
Futurism began in Italy where some artists tried to break from the past with art that showed moving things, often with angled or broken shapes.

1907-1920
Cubism was an important style of art, with Cubists showing things from several different angles at once on flat paper or canvases.

1915-1937
Suprematism was invented in Russia by Kazimir Malevich, an abstract style that focused on the paint rather than subjects. He often painted geometric shapes that seemed to float on the canvas. Constructivism followed, involving 3D abstract objects that influenced modern architecture and design.

1916-1924
Dada developed among artists and writers who were horrified by the First World War. The art often seemed to be about nonsense on purpose – because they thought the war did not make sense.

1917-1944
Neo-Plasticism was an abstract style, invented by Piet Mondrian and Theo van Doesburg. It was based on straight lines, right angles, primary colours and black and white.

1924-1950s
Surrealism was invented by writers, but artists soon began expressing the subconscious, dreams and emotions, sometimes using 'automatism' – drawing and painting without thinking consciously.

1945-1950s
Abstract Expressionism was an American art movement. Abstract Expressionists made large abstract art and included Jackson Pollock, Lee Krasner, Mark Rothko and Willem and Elaine de Kooning.

1956-1970
Pop art often used commercial art techniques and included common, everyday images, such as advertising, comics and mass-produced food.

1960s-21st century
Earth or land art uses the natural landscape for large structures. The artists are usually conscious of the environment and so draw attention to the land.

1960s-21st century
Conceptual art makes the idea the most important part of the artwork. Conceptual artists reacted against the high prices that many works of art sell for and aimed to make the viewer think.

1970s-21st century
Street art grew out of graffiti art, which was usually made by young artists who were protesting about something.

1970s-21st century
Performance art is made by artists doing things for audiences to watch and to encourage them to raise questions and concerns about society.

INDEX

FIND OUT MORE

Books

Art A Children's Encyclopedia, Susie Hodge and David Taylor, 2017, DK
Why is Art Full of Naked People? Susie Hodge, 2016, Thames & Hudson
Great Art in 30 Seconds: 30 Awesome Art Topics for Curious Kids, Susie Hodge, 2018, Ivy Kids
13 Art Movements Children Should Know, Brad Finger, 2014, Prestel
13 Art Techniques Children Should Know, Angela Wenzel, 2014, Prestel
13 Art Materials Children Should Know, Narcisa Marchioro, 2017, Prestel

Websites

www.bbc.co.uk/bitesize/topics/zsx6fg8
With links to other sites and videos about a range of art and art history.

www.tate.org.uk/kids
Some fun activities based on artists and art movements, plus interesting information.

www.ducksters.com/history/art/
Includes links to find out more about a range of art history topics.

b-inspiredmama.com/art-history-for-kids/
A fun alphabet of art, with information and varied activities about a range of art and artists.